The Art of Brand Narratives

A Guide to Elevating Your
Business through Storytelling

ANTHONY MALACHY

Table of content

CHAPTER ONE

CHAPTER TWO

CHAPTER THREE

CHAPTER FOUR

CHAPTER FIVE

CONCLUSION

CHAPTER ONE
Introduction

A compelling brand story is what distinguishes a company in a world full of noise and distraction. A compelling brand narrative has the ability to enthrall consumers, create emotional connections, and forge a distinctive identity that sets a company apart from the competitors. The Art of Brand Narratives is a thorough manual on the craft of corporate storytelling. It examines the essential components of a compelling brand story and offers useful advice for creating, reaching out to, and interacting with consumers. Anyone trying to promote their brand via the power of storytelling should read this book. The Art of Brand Narratives is your indispensable manual for crafting a narrative that enthralls, connects, and propels commercial success, whether you are just beginning to develop your brand narrative or want to revise and enhance an existing one.

The key benefits of creating a compelling brand story:

Differentiation: One of the main advantages of telling an engaging brand narrative is differentiation. In the crowded market of today, it's critical for a company to distinguish itself from the competition and stand out from the crowd. The values, purpose, and personality of a company may be communicated to consumers in a memorable and meaningful manner via a well-crafted brand narrative, which can aid in achieving this difference. The firm will develop as a result of its ability to stand out from the competition and win over new clients while retaining those it already has.

Increased Customer Engagement:

Another significant advantage of telling an engaging brand narrative is increased consumer interaction. A well-written tale has the ability to enthrall and engage viewers, creating emotional bonds that may improve client loyalty and advocacy. Customers are more inclined to interact with a brand, tell others about their experiences with it, and buy from it again if they feel a connection to it. Businesses may engage consumers in a more meaningful and impactful manner, which will eventually result in improved engagement and success, by developing a powerful brand narrative.

Improved Brand Awareness:

Improved brand awareness is a significant benefit of creating a compelling brand story. When a business has a strong and well-communicated brand story, it has the power to reach new audiences and raise awareness of its products or services. This can be achieved through various marketing channels, such as social media, advertising, and public relations, which can help spread the brand story and reach a wider audience. As brand awareness grows, so does the potential for increased customer engagement and sales, making it an important factor in driving business success. By investing in the creation and communication of a strong brand story, businesses can take a crucial step towards improving brand awareness and achieving their growth goals.

Increased Trust and Credibility: A firm may get several advantages by developing an engaging brand narrative, including improved credibility and trust. A well-written brand narrative may aid in creating a company's identity and letting consumers know about its values, purpose, and personality.

Customers are more likely to engage with a brand and see it as a dependable and trustworthy source when it has a clear and consistent message. This is crucial in the competitive market of today, where customers may choose from a variety of goods and services. A business may stand out from its rivals and establish a distinctive brand in the eyes of clients by creating an engaging tale.

A compelling brand narrative may also aid in establishing an emotional connection with clients. A business may build a feeling of community and generate a higher degree of engagement with its target market by appealing to the emotions and values of its consumers.

Enhanced Reputation:

An effective approach for increasing a company's reputation is a captivating brand narrative. It enables a company to separate itself from its rivals and create a distinctive and memorable brand identity by helping to generate a clear and consistent picture in the minds of consumers. In addition to appealing to customers' beliefs and aspirations, a well-crafted brand narrative has the power to inspire strong emotional bonds, fostering brand loyalty and commitment. Given that individuals prefer to recall and react favorably to companies with which they identify, this emotional connection may be especially potent.

Additionally, telling a captivating brand narrative helps support establishing credibility and trust with customers. Customers are more inclined to trust the quality and dependability of the goods or services given when they are aware of the company's beliefs and purpose. A firm may become a trusted source by developing a brand narrative that is consistent, open, and genuine. This is crucial in a time when customers are becoming more selective about the goods and services they purchase.

Finally, a compelling brand narrative may improve brand awareness and alter how people see a business. Customers are more likely to recall and identify a brand's narrative and values if they are acquainted with them, which increases brand recognition and preference. As a result, a firm may see increased sales and growth as well as an improvement in its standing as a valued and trustworthy brand.

Conclusion: By generating a distinctive and memorable brand identity, fostering consumer trust and credibility, raising brand awareness and favorable impression, and more, developing an engaging brand narrative may play a vital part in improving a company's image.

Increased Sales:

Yes, creating a memorable brand narrative may result in higher sales. A compelling brand narrative may help set a business apart from its rivals and increase client retention and recognition. Customers are more likely to pick a brand over rivals when they have an emotional connection to it and are aware of its values and purpose, which promotes customer loyalty and repeat business.

Furthermore, customers are more inclined to pick a brand for their purchases when they have confidence in it and see it as credible. Customers are more inclined to make purchases and refer a brand to others when they trust it and have faith in the excellence and dependability of its goods and services.

In conclusion, a strong brand identity, emotional ties with consumers, and trust-building relationships with them are all ways that a captivating brand narrative may spur sales growth.

CHAPTER TWO

Building Your Brand Narrative.

Developing a brand narrative entails writing a narrative that captures the essence of your company's brand and identifies its distinctive features and core values. These stages will assist you in developing your brand story.

Identify your brand's core values:

Building a powerful and engaging brand story requires taking the time to determine your business's key principles. Your brand's core principles form its basis and direct all business choices. Think about doing the following actions to determine your brand's key values:

Consider your company's mission: Consider your brand's objective and the principles you want it to uphold. This will assist you in identifying values that support the purpose and objectives of your brand.

Analyze the personality of your brand: Think about the personality, tone, and style of your brand. What characteristics do you want it to exhibit and what ideals does it embody?

Think about who you want to reach: Consider the values that matter to and what your target market is looking for in a brand.

Consider your brand's past: Consider the history of your brand and the principles that have shaped it over the years. What principles have endured over time, and what principles have changed?

Obtain input from key players: Find out what values your stakeholders—including staff, customers, and other stakeholders—connect with your brand. You may find values that are crucial to the success and reputation of your brand by using their insights.

Focus on the most important and significant principles for your brand after creating a list of your core beliefs. These have to be principles that excite you and are consistent with the vision and objectives of your brand.

You can develop an authentic and powerful brand story by having a clear knowledge of the key principles of your company. It will direct your brand choices and assist in creating a dependable and recognised brand identity.

Define your brand's mission:

Building a compelling brand story begins with defining your business's objective. The brand purpose outlines what your brand represents and why it was created, acting as a compass for all brand choices. Think about doing the following actions to identify your brand's mission:

Consider the reason for your brand's existence and the goals you have for it as a starting point.

Determine who your target market is: What demands will your brand satisfy, and who will gain from it? Establishing the objective of your brand requires an understanding of your target audience.

Think about your brand's core principles: Take into account the principles you wish to convey to clients via your brand.

Consider your rivals: Examine what makes your brand different from those of rivals and what special features and advantages it provides.

Keep it brief: Your brand's mission statement should be clear and simple. It must to make your brand's mission and objectives crystal clear and unforgettable.

Make it actionable: Your brand purpose should inspire action and decision-making rather than merely serving as a statement. Make sure it has significance and inspires your staff to fulfill the objectives of your brand.

Disseminate it: To make sure that everyone is on the same page and is aware of what your brand stands for, communicate your brand purpose to your staff, stakeholders, and consumers.

In addition to ensuring that every action made by the brand is in line with its purpose and values, having a well defined brand mission may assist build a strong and consistent brand identity. Additionally, it will assist consumers understand the core of your business and build a relationship that encourages engagement and loyalty.

Know your target audience:

Building a compelling brand story begins with knowing your target market. You may design your brand narrative to appeal to your target audience's requirements, values, and preferences in a manner that encourages participation. Take into account the following actions to understand your target market:

Conduct market research: To learn more about your target audience, use surveys, focus groups, and other research techniques.

Analyze your client information: Gain insights into the demographics, habits, and interests of your target audience by using data from your sales, customer service, and marketing initiatives.

Analyze your rivals: Consider your rivals' target markets and the products and services they are providing to them.

Look at the current clientele of your brand: Look into the reasons why the consumers who are already interacting with your brand do so.

Create buyer personas by creating thorough profiles of your target market using the information you have gathered. You will have a deeper understanding of their needs, drives, and actions as a result.

Stay up to date: To keep it current and correct, examine and refresh your knowledge of your target audience often.

You can develop a brand story that connects with your target market and promotes engagement and loyalty by knowing who they are. As a result, you'll be able to better fulfill their requirements and preferences with your marketing and sales efforts and make sure that your brand is well-positioned to flourish in your market.

Create a story arc:

In order to develop an engaging brand narrative, a story arc is essential. Your brand narrative is given shape and direction by a story arc, which also engages your target market. Take into account the following actions to develop a narrative arc:

Begin with a challenge: Introduce an issue or difficulty that your target customer confronts in your brand narrative.

Introduce your company as the remedy: Present your brand as the answer to the issue, and describe how it does so in a compelling and distinctive manner.

Highlight important qualities and advantages: Highlight the distinctive qualities and advantages of your brand that set it apart from the competition.

Focus on building emotional connections with your audience by using emotive storytelling to connect with and stir their emotions.

Display the outcomes Show the influence of your brand and how it has aided consumers in achieving their objectives and overcoming difficulties.

Call your audience to action at the end of your brand narrative to motivate them to take further action and interact with your brand.

Your target audience is more likely to get interested in and engaged with your brand and remember its distinctive value proposition if you develop a captivating narrative arc for it. A compelling narrative arc may help set your company apart from rivals and establish a bond with your target market that encourages advocacy and loyalty.

Use vivid language and imagery:

Making a captivating brand story requires the use of vivid language and images. Using vivid language and images makes your brand narrative come to life and better engages your target audience.

Think about the following advice to utilize vivid language and imagery:

Being descriptive can assist your target audience see and feel your brand narrative by using language that paints a picture in their minds.

Use sensory language to provide your target audience an immersive and unforgettable experience. Include language that plays on their five senses (sight, hearing, touch, taste, and smell).

Use metaphors and similes to enhance the vividness and recall of your brand's narrative.

Utilize dynamic imagery: To assist bring your brand's narrative to life, use photos that are eye-catching, vibrant, and colorful.

Be creative: Don't be scared to use innovative words and creative images. Your brand narrative will stand out and be more memorable as a result of this.

Your brand narrative will come to life and be more memorable and effective if you use vivid language and images. Additionally, it will help you connect emotionally with your target audience and better engage them.

Make it consistent:

Building a compelling brand story requires consistency. Your target audience will know what to anticipate from your brand if you maintain a consistent brand story, which also helps to increase brand awareness and trust. Think about taking the following actions to ensure consistency in your brand narrative:

Create a style manual: The tone, style, and message of your brand story should be outlined in a style guide.

Make sure your brand story is consistent across all touchpoints, such as your website, social media accounts, advertisements, and customer communications.

Train your staff: Make sure your team is aware of the brand's message and style guide so they know what is expected of them when they represent the company.

In order to maintain consistency, track and evaluate your brand story over time and make improvements as necessary.

Refresh frequently: To keep it current and consistent with your brand and your target audience, regularly examine and update your brand story.

A consistent brand story makes it easier for people to recognize and trust your company, and it also lets your target market know what to anticipate from you. In order to better engage and win over your target audience's loyalty, it also helps to develop a clear and cohesive brand message.

Test and refine:

A crucial stage in the creation of an engaging brand story is testing and improving your brand narrative. You can make sure that your brand story is persuasive and appealing to your target market by testing and improving it. If you want to test and improve your brand story, think about doing the following:

Test with a small group: To begin, test your brand story with a select group of stakeholders or clients. Then, get their input on how well it works.

Refine depending on input: Make necessary tweaks and revisions to your brand story as a result of the feedback you get to make it more persuasive and appealing to your target audience.

In order to determine how successfully your brand story is

connecting with your target audience, it is important to track engagement over time.

Iterate: Based on user input and engagement statistics, continuously iterate and improve your brand story.

Analyze outcomes: Monitor the impact of your brand story over time and tweak it as necessary to maintain its potency and appeal to your target market.

Your brand story may be improved and tested to assist you make sure it is compelling and appealing to your target market. Additionally, it enables you to develop your brand narrative over time and make it more compelling and effective.

CHAPTER THREE

Storytelling through Visuals.

Visual storytelling is a potent tool for engaging your target audience and bringing your brand's narrative to life. Visuals may enhance the impact and memorability of your brand narrative while also fostering an emotional connection with your target market. Adapt the following advice to your brand narrative if you want to incorporate visuals:

Use high-quality pictures: To increase the impact of your brand narrative, use visuals that are clear, crisp, and appealing.

Pick the proper images: Select images that support and enhance your brand's narrative by being meaningful and relevant to it.

Utilize a variety of visuals: To develop a compelling brand narrative, utilize a variety of visuals, such as photos, videos, and graphics.

Make your pictures simple to post on social media to assist your brand narrative go farther by ensuring that they are shareable.

To captivate your target audience and foster an emotional connection, use pictures to convey a tale that has a distinct beginning, middle, and finish.

Visual storytelling is a potent tool for engaging your target audience and bringing your brand's narrative to life. It may assist to strengthen the emotional connection between your target audience and your brand narrative, making it more memorable and compelling.

Power and potentials of visual storytelling :

When it comes to creating an engaging brand narrative, visual storytelling has enormous power and potential. The following are some of the main advantages of visual storytelling:

Increased engagement: By enhancing engagement and making your brand's narrative more memorable and compelling, visual storytelling may help you forge a closer bond with your target audience.

Emotional connection: Visuals may aid in creating an emotional bond with your target market, enhancing the impact and engagement of your brand narrative.

Better understanding: Using visuals may make difficult ideas or concepts easier for your target audience to comprehend.

Increased reach: Because visual storytelling is so simple to share on social media and other platforms, it may assist to increase the audience for your brand narrative.

Differentiation: By bringing your brand narrative to life in a distinctive and powerful manner, visual storytelling may assist to distinguish your business and make it stand out in a crowded market.

When it comes to creating an engaging brand narrative, visual storytelling has enormous power and potential. You may improve engagement, create an emotional connection with your target audience, and set your company apart in a congested market by including graphics into your brand story.

CHAPTER FOUR

Storytelling through Content Marketing.

The efficacy of content marketing may be considerably increased by using the potent instrument of storytelling. You may capture your audience and increase the impact and memory of your brand's message by including aspects of storytelling into your marketing approach.

You may establish an emotional connection with your target audience by using a well-written tale. People are more likely to remember a message and the brand behind it when they are engaged in the narrative.

Storytelling may also help your brand become more approachable and enticing to your audience by humanizing it.

Storytelling may be included into your content marketing efforts in a variety of ways. You may develop a tale around the background, goals, and principles of your company, or you can utilize characters and a story to highlight the characteristics and advantages of your goods. You may use storytelling to highlight client testimonials and describe client experiences.

Some of the most popular mediums for storytelling in content marketing are blogs, videos, and social media postings. You may develop information that is both enjoyable and educational by employing imaginative and captivating language and imagery. You may develop a strong brand personality, raise brand recognition, and build credibility and trust with your audience by using this kind of material.

It's crucial to keep in mind that storytelling encompasses more than merely producing material for entertainment purposes. To engage your audience and promote business outcomes, include narrative in your content marketing strategy. It is vital to coordinate your narrative efforts with your overall marketing goals and objectives because of this.

As a result, using storytelling in content marketing may be a very successful approach to convey your brand's message, values, and services in a distinctive and compelling manner. You can build a stronger relationship with your audience, raise brand recognition, and promote business success by using the power of storytelling.

Power and potentials of storytelling through Content Marketing.

A target audience may be captivated, engaged, and influenced by using storytelling in content marketing. Some of the opportunities for storytelling in content marketing are listed below:

Emotional connection: Storytelling helps companies to emotionally connect with their audience, increasing the message's impact and memorability.

Brand humanization: A brand may be made more relevant and engaging to the public by using stories.

Storytelling may improve audience participation, which in turn promotes brand recognition and patron loyalty.

Differentiation: By developing a distinctive brand personality and voice, storytelling may assist a company in standing out from its rivals.

Storytelling is a great strategy for brand recall and retention since it is more probable that people will remember stories than facts and data.

Versatility across platforms: Storytelling may be utilized successfully on a range of platforms and media types, including blogs, videos, social media, and more.

Increased conversion: By gaining the audience's confidence and credibility via storytelling, it becomes simpler to offer goods and services.

In conclusion, using storytelling in content marketing has the ability to significantly improve a brand's marketing initiatives and provide profitable outcomes. Brands can produce content that is memorable and effective by using the power of narrative, which will drive engagement, brand recognition, and eventually sales.

CHAPTER FIVE
Measuring the Success of Your Storytelling Strategy.

It's critical to evaluate the efficacy of your narrative approach in order to make the required adjustments. When determining the effectiveness of your storytelling efforts, take into account the following important metrics:

Measure the likes, comments, shares, and views that your narrative material has received. High levels of engagement show that your tales are having an impact on your audience.

Track the traffic brought about by your narrative material, including the number of visitors, page views, and time spent on the website. Traffic growth may be a sign that your articles are raising awareness of your company.

Conversion rate: Keep track of your narrative content's conversion rate, including the quantity of leads and purchases it produces. Higher conversion rates may be a sign that your tales are successfully highlighting the benefits of your goods and services.

Brand Awareness: Keep tabs on how your narrative is affecting brand recognition, including mentions in media, placement in search results, and social media followers. Increased brand recognition may be a sign that your tales are successfully conveying the message and values of your company.

Customer Loyalty: Evaluate how your narrative affects consumer loyalty, including return business and lifetime value. Customer loyalty that has increased may be a sign that your tales are establishing a deep emotional connection with your audience.

Return on Investment (ROI): To determine the ROI of your storytelling efforts, compare the expense of developing and disseminating your tales with the income produced. A high return on investment (ROI) might be a sign that your storytelling technique is cost-effective.

In conclusion, it is critical to evaluate the efficacy of your storytelling approach in order to make the required adjustments. You may assess the effects of your storytelling efforts on engagement, traffic, conversion, brand recognition, customer loyalty, and return on investment by monitoring five important measures.

CONCLUSION

A thorough manual for developing and putting into practice effective storytelling techniques in the context of branding and marketing is called "The Art of Brand Narratives." The book examines the effectiveness of storytelling and how it may strengthen brand message and develop stronger emotional connections with customers. It provides rules for assessing the effectiveness of storytelling activities as well as helpful advice and ideas for creating appealing brand tales.

Anyone wishing to strengthen their brand via storytelling will find a lot of knowledge and inspiration in this book. Whether you're an experienced marketer or you're just getting started, "The Art of Brand Narratives" is a great book that will teach you the fundamentals of powerful storytelling and how to use it to achieve business goals.

To sum up, "The Art of Brand Narratives" is a must-read for anybody hoping to use the power of storytelling to create a powerful and enduring brand. This book gives you the skills and expertise you need to create compelling brand narratives that connect with your target audience and promote commercial success, whether you're working on a brand refresh or beginning from scratch.

www.ingramcontent.com/pod-product-compliance
Lightning Source LLC
Chambersburg PA
CBHW070321220526
45465CB00013B/2004